152.4

‖‖‖ ‖‖‖‖‖‖‖‖‖ ‖‖‖‖‖‖‖‖‖ ‖‖‖
W9-AYA-620

THE POWER OF
INTEGRITY

Featuring the story of J.C. Penney

Authors
Phyllis Colonna
Della Mae Rasmussen

Art Illustrator
Stephen P. Krause

Editor, Layout and Research
Beatrice W. Friel

THE POWER OF INTEGRITY

Featuring the story of J.C. Penney

Advisors
Paul and Millie Cheesman
Mark Ray Davis
Rodney L. Mann, Jr.
Roxanne Shallenberger
Dale T. Tingey

Publisher
Steven R. Shallenberger

Director and Correlator
Lael J. Woodbury

AN EAGLE SYSTEMS
INTERNATIONAL
PUBLICATION

ANTIOCH, CALIFORNIA

The Power of Integrity
Copyright © 1981 by
PowerTales
Eagle Systems International
P.O. Box 1229
Antioch, California 94509

ISBN: 0-911712-85-2

Library of Congress Catalog No.: 81-50390

First Edition

Lithographed in USA by
COMMUNITY PRESS, INC.

Dedicated to children everywhere in the hope that they will realize the importance of integrity in their everyday dealings with others.

J.C. PENNEY

James Cash Penney was born on a farm near Hamilton, Missouri, on 16 September 1875. He was the seventh of twelve children born to an impoverished Baptist preacher.

Jim's parents were religious, well-educated, and cultured. When Jim was four years old the family moved to Hamilton to enable the children to go to school. His father felt a practical education was equally important, and gave his children many opportunities to learn.

Jim grew up to be a hard worker, finding real joy in good, honest work. In 1895, when Jim was nineteen, his father arranged for him to work in the store of J.M. Hale. There, while earning a meager salary, Jim learned the fundamentals of honest business. The faith that his father showed in him sustained him through trying times. As his self-respect grew, he enjoyed meeting and selling to customers, going to great lengths to please them.

Feeling that he must "more than earn every penny of his pay," Jim worked hard for long hours, which took its toll on his health. His doctor advised him to go West, for there was danger that his "persistent bronchial cold" might turn into tuberculosis. Jim packed his bags and went to Colorado, finding work in a Denver dry goods store. Not feeling in harmony with some of the store's dealings and not enjoying big city life, however, he moved to Longmont, a small town north of Denver. After an unsuccessful venture in a meat market, Jim was given an opportunity to work in a store in Evanston, Wyoming. On 24 August 1899 in Cheyenne, Wyoming, he married Berta Hess, a girl he had courted while living in Longmont.

In 1902 Jim and Berta arrived in Kemmerer, Wyoming, where he was to be a partner in a new store. Jim made shelves and a counter for the store from empty merchandise crates. He and Berta lived in an attic room above the store and used packing crates to make their furniture. Jim and Berta worked long hours in their "Golden Rule" store. The store opened at seven in the morning and did not close until late at night when no more customers could be seen on the streets. Their first baby slept in a crate under the counter while Berta worked in the store. Soon Jim was able to pay off his entire loan on the store, and he became a full partner. In 1907 Jim's partners, Callahan and Johnson, offered to lend Jim the money to buy them out. Thus at 32 Jim was the proud owner of three dry goods stores. He continued opening stores and taking in new partners as his former partners had done with him. By 1910 Jim had a chain of fourteen stores.

Jim moved his wife and two little sons to Salt Lake City in 1901. It was here the following Christmas that Berta died of pneumonia. Jim sank into a deep despair and walked for hours deep into the night. Then he tried to lose himself in his work. His business grew by leaps and bounds, but he still felt a deep sense of loss. It was on a trip to the Holy Land that he finally came to the realization that "it is useless to run away from life."

In 1912 the name of his stores was changed from "Golden Rule" to "J.C. Penney Company." Then in 1917 Jim went back to school. After 18 months of intensive study, Jim started an educational program for his organization.

In 1919 Jim married Mary Kimball, and they had one son. Mary died when her son was very small.

Later Jim married Caroline Autenreith and they had two daughters. In 1925 the Penney foundation was set up, and in 1927 the old partnership gave way to a profit-sharing plan.

When the depression of 1929 came, Jim's fortune of forty million dollars was practically wiped out. At the age of 56 he was flat broke, but with hard work and determination he fought his way through the depression and on through the war years.

As Jim was rebuilding his fortune, he was deeply concerned with spiritual values rather than "treasures on earth." He had many speaking engagements throughout the country on "The Application of Christian Principles in Business."

Jim was active in company affairs until a few months before his death. Of his success he said: "This company's success is due to the application of the golden rule to every individual, the public, and all of our activities." He died in New York in 1971 at the age of ninety-five.

Hello!

Have you ever said, "I wish I had a million dollars!" I'll bet you have, and I'll bet most of your friends have said the same thing. But how many people do you know who really *have* a million dollars? What makes them different? Why do their wishes come true while other people only talk about their wishes?

My name is Reggie Ruler. I want to tell you about a man who learned to make his wishes come true—a man named James Cash Penney. When Jim was a young boy, he was as poor as any young boy could be; but when he grew up, he had more than a million dollars. In fact, he had many times a million dollars!

But there is something even more important than that. Jim earned all his money without ever losing his integrity.

Now I know what you're thinking: *"Integrity!* What kind of a word is that! I can't even pronounce it. Am I supposed to know what it means?"

I admit that it's a hard word. As a matter of fact, some people live all their lives without learning what it means. But others, like Jim Penney, learn very young.

Having integrity means being honest, fair, and sincere at all times. It means never taking advantage of someone else to get something for yourself. Having integrity means having a firm set of rules to measure yourself by.

But let's see how Jim Penney learned to understand the meaning of integrity.

— TRUE INTEGRITY

— MOST HONEST

— HONEST

— ALMOST HONEST

— NOT HONEST

Jim was born in 1875 and grew up on a large farm on the prairie near Hamilton, Missouri. In many ways his life was hard. He had eleven brothers and sisters, and his family didn't have very much money. Everyone had to work hard to plant and harvest the fields, take care of the animals, and do all the other farm and household chores.

Jim's parents were unusual for people living in the rough frontier country of Missouri. Education and proper behavior were important to them. They loved to read books and discuss ideas.

Jim's father graduated from college at the age of seventeen. He had many unique ways of teaching his children the things he thought were important. He especially wanted them to know how to think for themselves and to be able to talk about their ideas with other people.

He enjoyed finding fun ways to teach these things. Sitting by the fire in the evening, he would often say to one of the children, "Let's have a debate." Jim was always eager, even though he knew his father would probably win. "You're a much better debator than I am, but I don't care," Jim would say. "You know how to make losing almost as much fun as winning."

Mr. Penney would choose an idea or event and ask, "Do you want to be the Yes side or the No side?" After Jim had decided, his father would take the other side, and the family would be treated to a lively discussion.

Jim liked talking to his mother, too. He often went into the warm kitchen while she was cooking dinner or ironing great stacks of clothes for her large family. He enjoyed sitting in the kitchen and watching his mother work. Almost always there was a kettle of hearty soup simmering at the back of the stove or a spicy pie baking in the oven.

"Don't you wish we had more money, Mother?" he asked. "Then you wouldn't have to work so hard." Jim knew that when his mother was growing up in Kentucky she had been very rich and hadn't had to work at all. But their frontier farm in Missouri did not make much money.

Mrs. Penney smiled. She seldom seemed tired or discouraged. "It's true we don't have much money, Jim," she said. "But we have many things other people would be glad to have."

"Like our bluegrass farm?" he asked.

"Like our farm and our warm home and the good things to eat that we grow for ourselves," she answered. She gave Jim a warm hug. "Don't forget that we have each other, too." she said.

Whenever he could, Jim went with his father to town or on other errands. Once they took their cattle all the way to Chicago to sell. Jim never forgot the exciting train ride and all the different things he saw in the busy city.

He liked watching his father conduct business with the other men, but his favorite times were when the two of them were alone. Then his father talked to him about the things he believed in most. Quite often he talked about integrity.

"Do you know what I want people to remember about me after I die?" Mr. Penney once asked his son. Jim shook his head. "When people pass my grave I want them to say, 'There lies an honest man,'" Mr. Penney answered. "If they can say that, that's the highest praise I'd ever ask for."

18

Jim admired his father, but sometimes he wondered if he could ever grow up to be as strong and as smart as his father. Mr. Penney seemed to see farther into things than other people. Once he made up his mind about what was right, he never backed down.

THINK ABOUT IT

1. How did Mr. Penney teach Jim about integrity?
2. Think of someone you know who has integrity.

JIM BEGINS TO EARN HIS OWN MONEY

At first some of his father's decisions seemed very hard to Jim.

One night Mr. Penney called his son aside to talk to him. "Jim, you're eight years old now," he said. "I think you're big enough to start buying your own clothes. What do you think?"

Jim was so surprised he could hardly think at all. "Clothes cost a lot of money," he said at last. "I don't have any money."

"No one has any money until he finds a way to earn it," his father answered.

"But I don't know any way to earn money," Jim blurted out.

"You're a bright boy, son." Mr. Penney said. "You can come up with an idea if you think about it. That's what your brothers did. That's what I did, too."

Jim thought of the book and the new pocketknife he wanted to buy. He looked at his old shoes, each one with a hole in the bottom. "Will you buy me one more pair of shoes first?" he asked hopefully.

Mr. Penney shook his head. His voice was kind but very firm. "No, Jim, I won't be able to do that," he said. "It's time you started depending on yourself. When you get the hang of it, I shouldn't wonder if you'll feel quite proud buying what you need with your own money."

At first Jim was so worried he thought he would toss and turn all night. But he had worked hard that day, and soon he was fast asleep.

First thing next morning Jim jumped out of bed and ran to talk to his mother. She was fixing breakfast at the kitchen stove. "Father says it's time for me to buy my own clothes," he said worriedly.

Mrs. Penney smiled. "You must feel very grown up," she answered.

"But I don't know any way to earn money," he said.

"Oh, you'll find a way if you think about it," his mother said confidently.

Jim ate his breakfast and went outside to find his brothers. But no matter how many people he talked to, they all told him the same thing: "You'll find a way to earn money if you just keep thinking about it."

For several days Jim thought and thought, but no ideas came to him. Meanwhile he found odd jobs to do for a nickel or a few pennies. He collected horseshoe nails from the blacksmith's floor, helped in the hayfields, drove the cows out to pasture for the neighbors, and cut grass and delivered packages for the women in town. One woman tried to pay him with cookies instead of money. Jim was polite but firm. "We have cookies at home," he said. Part of integrity is standing up for what is right and fair for yourself. He knew the cookies would taste good, but they would not help him buy new shoes.

Little by little the money added up. Finally Jim had enough to buy his first pair of shoes. They were cheap and ugly, but they didn't have holes in the bottoms. Most important, he still had money left over.

He was still looking for a good way to earn money. He knew he could never buy everything he needed by running errands. Then one day the idea he had been waiting for came to him. "I'll buy a baby pig!" he thought excitedly. "I can feed it and take care of it myself, and when it's grown, I'll sell it."

Soon he was putting his plan into action. He bought a small pig from one of his neighbors. He even found a way to get free food. "My pig likes to eat peelings and leftover food," he told each of his neighbors. "If you'll let me have the garbage out of your kitchen, I'll come and take it away every day. I'll wash the garbage buckets, too, and bring them back shining clean."

28

The neighbors thought this was a great plan. They were glad Jim was doing what they didn't like to do themselves. Jim thought it was a great plan, too. His pig grew fast and sold for a good profit. He decided to use this money to buy twelve more baby pigs. Soon they were growing as fast as the first one.

But Jim's father decided it was time to have another talk about integrity. "I'm afraid you'll have to sell your pigs," he said.

"But they are not ready!" Jim answered. "I won't make nearly as much money if I sell them now! Let me wait a few months."

"I'm sorry," his father said firmly, "all the neighbors are complaining about the noise and the smell. One pig was all right, but twelve pigs are too many, especially now that they're getting so big. Do you think it's right to make all the neighbors suffer so you can earn extra money?"

After he thought about it for awhile, Jim decided it probably wasn't right. He sold the pigs before they were fully grown. He didn't make the hundreds of dollars he had hoped for, but he did make $60. That was more than he had ever made before. He decided he liked finding ways to earn money.

"I've decided to go to the sale and buy a horse," he told his father one day. "If I buy a mare with a young colt, I can keep her and sell the colt when it's grown. She'll have more colts, so I'll have a horse of my own and I'll make money, too!"

"That sounds like a good idea," his father said. "Be careful that you get a good horse though. Remember that horses you can buy cheap usually have something wrong with them."

"Aren't you coming with me?" Jim asked surprised. "No one can fool you about horses."

"I can come if you want me to," his father answered. "How much will you pay me for my advice?"

"Pay you!" Jim asked, shocked.

"I had to learn everything I know through study and hard experience, son," he said. "If you want the benefit of what I've learned, you should be willing to pay for it. That's part of having integrity."

"I think I can pick out my own horse," Jim said stiffly, and he left for the sale. Soon he returned home, proudly leading a beautiful mare with a young colt.

But that night the mare kicked so hard she broke all the boards out of her stall. No matter where Jim put her, she kicked the pen to pieces. Finally he had to sell her for less than he had paid.

"Well, horse trading isn't learned all in a minute, son," his father told him with a smile. "Next time you'll know one more thing to look for."

Jim found many different ways to earn money, but he still had some hard lessons to learn about integrity.

Mr. Penney wanted all his sons to learn to be good farmers, so he gave each of them a few acres where they could plant anything they wanted. Jim decided he would use his four acres to grow watermelons. They were easy to take care of and would sell for a good price. At the end of every summer the county fair was held in Hamilton. Jim knew all the people would be hot and thirsty at the fair, and when people are hot and thirsty nothing tastes better than watermelon.

Jim's melons grew even bigger and better than he had expected. The week before they were harvested, he and his dog sat in the field every night to keep the boys from Hamilton from taking a few home. Bright and early on the first day of the fair he hitched up his horse and wagon and loaded the juicy melons. He sold some of them in the streets of the town. Then he pulled his wagon as close as he could to the fairgrounds entrance.

Soon he was doing a booming business. Suddenly his father was standing in front of the wagon, his face looking very angry.

"Pick up and go home," he told Jim sternly. "You're disgracing the whole family."

Jim did as he was told, but he was not happy. He felt ashamed and embarrassed. He wondered what he had done to make his father so angry. He felt angry, too. He had been making a lot of money selling melons.

"Don't you know what you were doing?" his father asked when they got home. "People who sell things inside the fairgrounds pay money for that privilege. It's called a concession, and it costs them a good price."

"But I wasn't inside the fairgrounds!" Jim blurted out.

"That's right." his father said. "But you were just as close as you could get. You were taking trade away from the ones inside without paying on an equal basis with them. That's unfair dealing, son. You should know that by now."

"Pa, I didn't even know about the concessions," Jim said. He still felt his father was too harsh in his judgment.

"Well, you know about them now," his father answered sternly. "Don't ever let me see a son of mine taking advantage of others for his own benefit. Think about it."

Jim did think about it. He thought about it so much that the lesson his father taught him became a part of his life for as long as he lived. He was learning to understand the meaning of integrity; he was getting a firm set of rules to measure himself by.

THINK ABOUT IT

1. Why do you think Jim's father insisted that Jim begin to earn his own money?
2. How would the world be better if everyone had integrity?
3. How can *you* show that you are a person with integrity?

Jim helped with the farm work until he graduated from high school. However, he never had the interest in farming that his brothers and sisters had. One day his father called him in for a talk. "I don't think you will ever be happy farming," he told Jim. "I know you have a good head for buying and selling. Yesterday I talked to my friend Mr. Hale. He says you can work in his store for a year to learn his ways of doing business. I think you would be wise to take the job."

"How much will he pay?" Jim asked.

"Well, he already has all the clerks he needs," Mr. Penney answered. "He is only letting you work there as a special favor to me. He will pay you $2.27 a month."

"Only $2.27 a month!" Jim cried. "Pa! I can make $25 a month delivering things in my wagon!"

"That's true, son, but think about this," his father told him patiently. "In ten years you'd still be delivering things for $25 a month. On the other hand, Mr. Hale is one of the smartest and most respected businessmen in Hamilton. If you learn the dry goods business from him, who knows how much you can benefit from the education."

Jim thought about that idea for several minutes. He had often heard his father say, "I don't think a man can make a million dollars and keep his integrity." Jim wanted to make a million dollars, and he wanted to do it in a way his father could be proud of. Mr. Hale knew how to make money, and he still had people's respect.

But when he reported for work he found that low wages were only the beginning of his problems. The other clerks didn't want him to work there. For one thing, Jim was much younger than they were and they didn't think he knew anything. For another, Jim didn't look very good to them. Since he had to buy his own clothes, he usually bought the cheapest ones he could find. The other clerks were well-dressed and careful of their appearance. Whenever they could, they played tricks on him. They found ways to steal Jim's customers from him and make the sales themselves. Jim was most unhappy.

He didn't know how to stop the clerks from being rude, so he spent most of his time in the back room working with the stock. Soon he knew more about the stock than anyone else in the store. But he still wasn't making any sales, and he knew Mr. Hale wouldn't keep a salesclerk who couldn't sell anything—not even for $2.27 a month.

One day Jim decided he had been hiding in the back room long enough. He banged his fist on the counter. "Those clerks can't make a fool out of me unless I let them!" he said angrily. "No more excuses! I'll go out there and show them what kind of person Jim Penney really is."

From then on Jim worked with pride and good humor, no matter what anyone else did. When one of the other clerks stole one of his customers, he found a way to bring the customer back again. Soon he was one of the best salesmen in the store. In fact, at the end of the year Mr. Hale offered him ten times as much money if he would stay another year.

But Jim hadn't been feeling well, and one day he went to see a doctor. "I'm afraid I have bad news for you," the doctor said. "You'll have to move away from Hamilton. This climate and working indoors for long hours aren't good for you. If you value your health, go out West where you can get lots of fresh air and sunshine."

Jim was very sad to leave his home and family, but he packed up his few belongings and got on the train. First he went to Evanston, Wyoming, but he thought there were too many people in that growing city. He moved to Longmont, Colorado, a town more like Hamilton.

It was hard finding a job in a place where no one knew him. It was even harder finding a job where he could keep his integrity. He quit working at one store because the owner kept cheating people on the price of socks. He lost business at another store because he wouldn't bribe one of the town's most important customers to buy from him.

"What's the matter with you?" one of his friends asked. "You had better learn to go along with what other people want if you expect to make money."

"I want to give people good service," Jim said. "I want to give them good products for a fair price, too. But I can't go along with things I know are wrong just because someone wants me to. Even if it means I never have a job that pays well."

But people were beginning to know Jim in the small town, and they admired the way he wanted to live his life. That didn't stop them from teasing him, but secretly they respected his ideas.

Finally one of the storekeepers, Mr. Callahan, gave him a part-time job for the holidays. Jim did so well that when the holidays were over, Mr. Callahan didn't want him to leave.

"My partner, Guy Johnson, and I have another store in Wyoming," Mr. Callahan said. "Will you work for us there? We will make you our manager."

"Indeed I will!" Jim said. "How soon can I start?"

Jim was such a good manager of one store that soon Callahan and Johnson made him manager of three stores. Then they made him a full partner. In fact, after a few years they sold Jim their share in the stores, and Jim became owner of all three stores!

But that was only the beginning of Jim's success. He had learned how to earn money and use it wisely. Best of all, he had learned how to earn money without losing his integrity. He had measured up to the rules he had set for himself.

Many people came to talk to him. "What is the secret of your success?" they asked.

"Hard work is the first secret," Jim explained. "I work hard to give people the best service I can, and they appreciate my help."

"The second secret is, always be fair," he continued. "I give people the best quality for the lowest price I can. They know I never try to cheat them, so they come back again and again. They bring their friends, too."

"The third secret is, believe in other people and help them get ahead too," he said. "I always look for other people who have integrity. When I find them, I tell them, 'If you will work hard I will make you a partner and help you open a new store.' That way I help them make money, and they help me make money at the same time."

Jim's ideas worked so well that soon there were J.C. Penney stores all over the West.

In fact, in 1923 Jim bought his 500th store. And do you know which store it was? It was Mr. Hale's store in Hamilton, Missouri—the store where Jim had worked as a young boy.

There was a big celebration in Hamilton the day the J.C. Penney store opened. All the townspeople were proud of Jim and his success. Mr. Hale was proud of him, too.

"Well, Jim, you're a wealthy man now," Mr. Hale said. "It's hard to believe you were once a bashful young salesclerk. I'm sorry your father isn't still here. He'd be pleased to see how well you learned your lessons from him."

"I'm sorry he isn't here, too," Jim said. "I'd like to thank him for teaching me to work hard and always think about the right thing to do. I'd like to thank him for teaching me how important it is to be honest and fair. I'd like to tell him. 'Look, Pa! It *is* possible to earn a million dollars and keep your integrity.' "